These Are My Senses

What Can I Hear?

Joanna Issa

Heinemann
LIBRARY
Chicago, Illinois

Edited by Siân Smith
Designed by Richard Parker and Peggie Carley
Picture research by Tracy Cummins
Production by Victoria Fitzgerald
Originated by Capstone Global Library Ltd

Library of Congress Cataloging-in-Publication Data
Cataloging-in-publication information is on file with the Library of Congress.
ISBN 978-1-4846-0433-5 (paperback)
ISBN 978-1-4846-0446-5 (eBook PDF)

Image Credits
Alamy: Francois Werli, 7, Tetra Images, 17; Dreamstime: Carlosphotos, 8, 21 (left); Getty Images: Geri Lavrov, cover, lend Images - JGI/Jamie Grill, 10, Yang Liu, 9; Shutterstock: aceshot1, 12, Borislav Borisov, 6, 21 (right), 22 (right), back cover, Damien Richard, 14, Digital Storm, 4, 22 (left), jctabb, 16, 20 (right), Kalmatsuy Tatyana, 15, Lisajsh, 13, marco mayer, 5, Martin Novak, 19, Olly, 11, Sergey Lavrentev, 18, 20 (left)

Printed in the United States 5972

Contents

What Can I Hear?

I hear a **loud** siren.

I have to cover my ears.

I hear a **quiet** sound.

A bird is quiet.

I hear fireworks.

I have to cover my ears.

I hear a quiet sound.

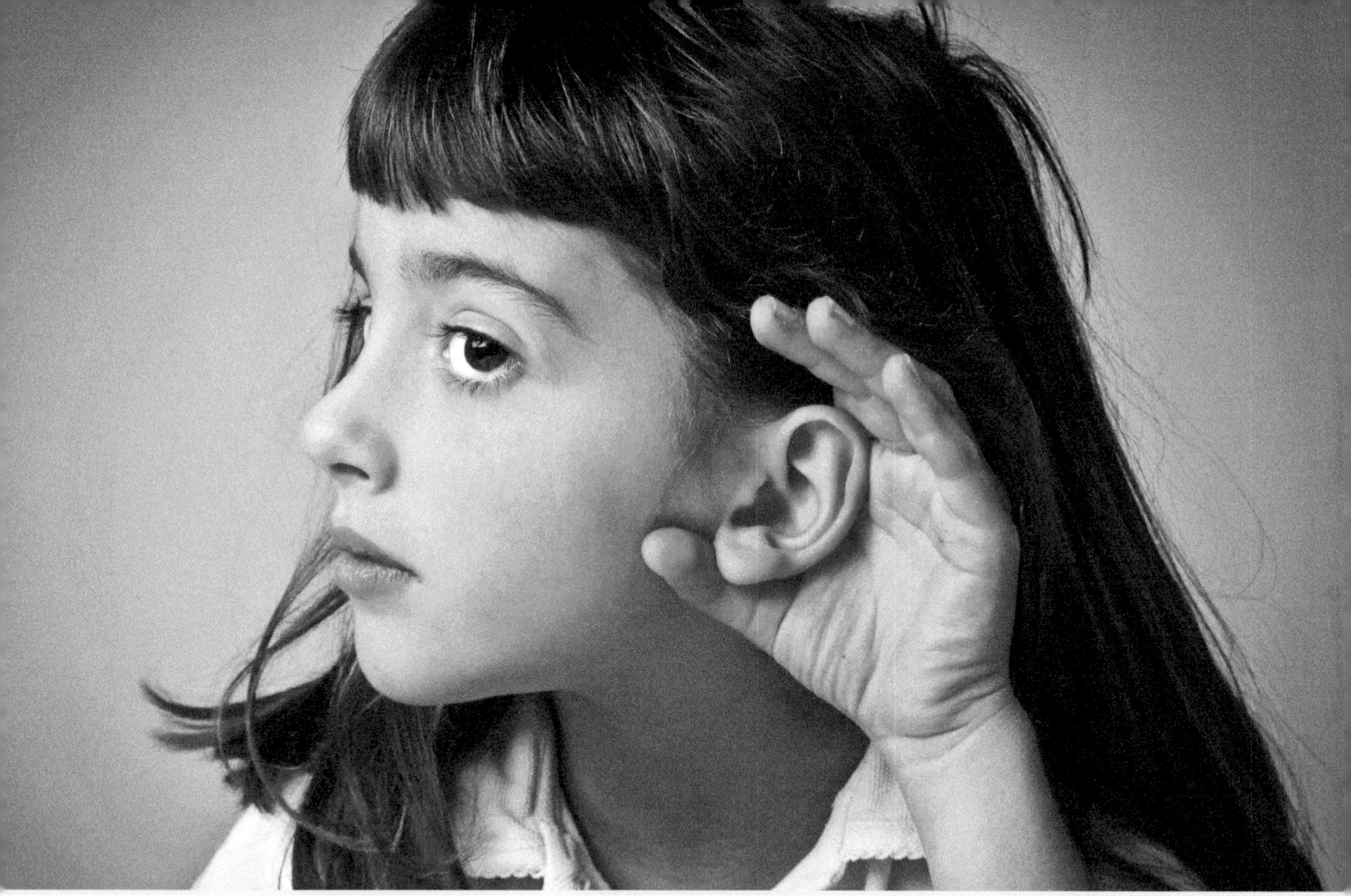

Rain is quiet.

I hear a drum.

I have to cover my ears.

I hear a quiet sound.

A cat is quiet.

I hear thunder.

I have to cover my ears.

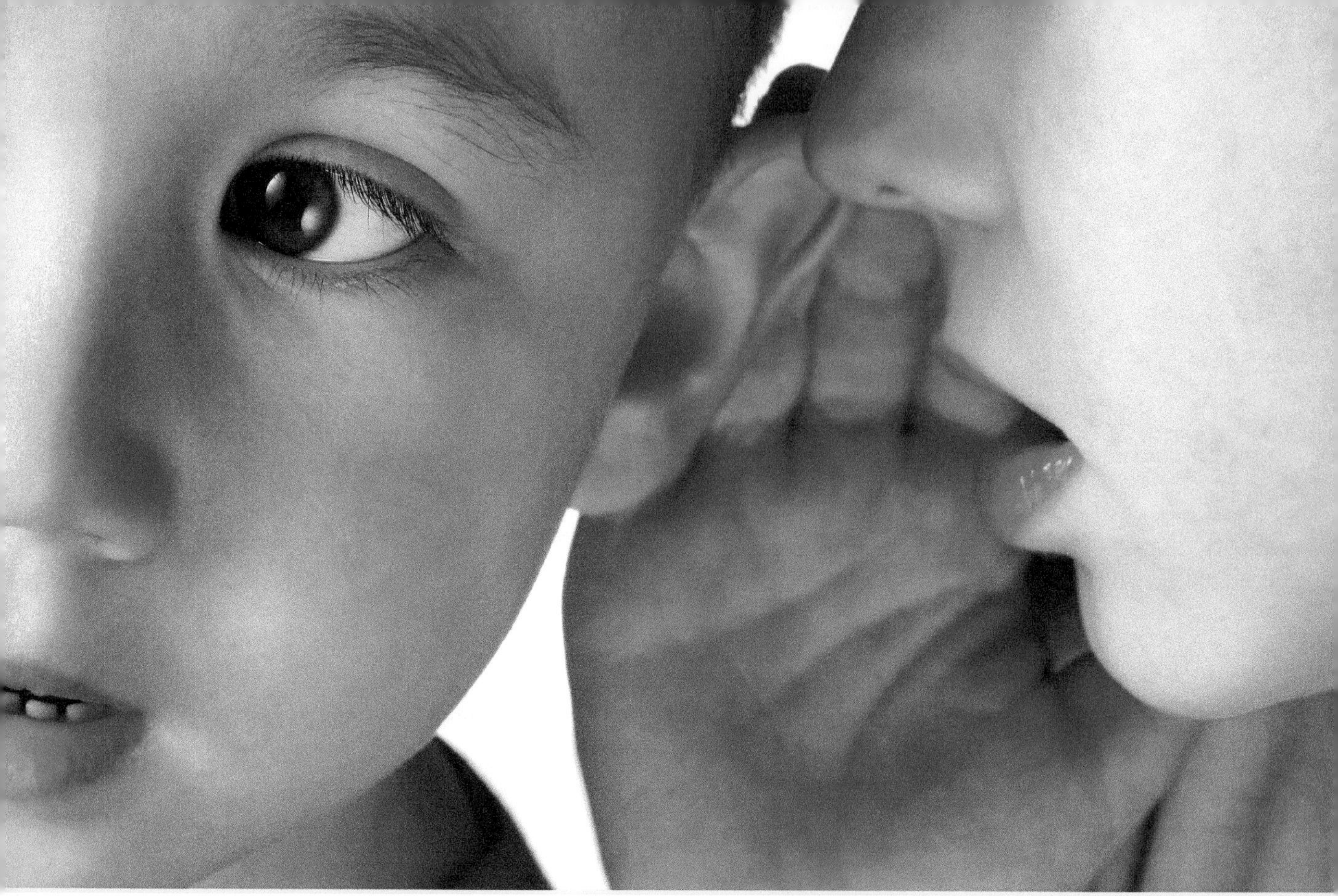

I hear a quiet sound.

A whisper is quiet.

Quiz: Spot the Difference

Can you find the loud sounds?

The thunder and the fireworks are loud.
The whisper and the bird are quiet.

Picture Glossary

loud

quiet

Index

Notes For Teachers and Parents

BEFORE READING

Building background:

Have children close their eyes and imagine a plane flying overhead. Would they call this sound loud or quiet? Then have them rub their hands gently on their shirt sleeves. Is the sound loud or quiet? Ask children how they hear sounds.

AFTER READING

Recall and reflection:

What sounds are loud? (siren, fireworks, drum, thunder) What sounds are quiet? (a bird singing, a cat purring, a whisper) What do the children in the book do when they hear loud sounds? What do we have to do to hear quiet sounds?

Sentence knowledge:

Ask children to look at page 13. How many sentences are on this page?
How can they tell?

Word knowledge (phonics):

Encourage children to point at the word *hear* on page 4. Sound out the two phonemes in the word *h/ear*. Ask children to sound out each phoneme as they point at the letters and then blend the sounds together to make the word *hear*. Challenge them to say some words that rhyme with *hear.* (ear, deer, gear, near)

Word recognition:

Have children point to the word *sound* on page 10.
On what other page can they find this word? (page 14)

EXTENDING IDEAS

Put some percussion instruments on a table. (tambourine, drum, cymbals, maraca) Let children listen to the sounds of each instrument and talk about whether the sound is loud or quiet. Cover up the instruments. Choose a child from the group, and tell the others to cover their eyes. Remove one of the instruments and ask the child to play the instrument. Can the rest of the class guess what instrument is being played? Tell the child to play the instrument very quietly at first and then to gradually get louder and louder. Do the other children need to cover their ears?

In This Book

Topic

hearing and senses

Sentence stems

1. I hear a loud ________.
2. I ________ cover my ears.
3. ________ is quiet.

High-frequency words

a

have

I

is

my

to